4 SIGNIFICANT SHIFTS IN GLOBAL POWER DYNAMICS

Knowing the factors behind that shift

BY

JOHN DAVIDSON

TABLE OF CONTENT

ABOUT THE AUTHOR

INTRODUCTION

JOHN DAVIDSON is a political writer who writes both fiction and nonfiction works.an investigative reporter who regularly writes on trending politics, government and history.he is one of the most influential public intellectuals in the world and one of the most often cited scholarship modern history.

Introduction:

The world has seen a significant shift in global power dynamics over the last few decades. This shift has been marked by the gradual decline of Western powers' dominance and the rise of developing nations in Asia, Africa, and Latin America. This shift will have far-reaching consequences for the global economy, politics, and security. In this essay, we will look at the factors driving this shift in global power dynamics, its impact on the world order, and possible future scenarios.

CHAPTER 1

The Rise of China.

One of the most significant drivers of the shift in global power dynamics has been China's rise as an economic and military power. Over the last three decades, China's economy has grown at an annual rate of 10% on average, making it the world's second-largest. This expansion has been fueled by several factors, including low labor costs, government support for industries, and infrastructure investment. China has also made significant investments in its military capabilities, such as the development of advanced weapons and the modernization of its armed forces. This has enabled China to challenge the United States' traditional military dominance in the Asia-Pacific region.

CHAPTER 2

The Decline of Western Powers

Another significant factor in the shift in global power dynamics has been the decline of Western powers, particularly the United States. The United States has faced economic challenges such as high debt levels and an expanding trade deficit. Its political and military influence has also been weakened by the wars in Iraq and Afghanistan, as well as its inability to resolve Middle Eastern conflicts. The European Union has also faced economic challenges, such as Greece's debt crisis and

the refugee crisis. This
has weakened the EU's
global political and
economic influence.

CHAPTER 3

The Rise of Developing Nations.

The rise of developing countries, particularly in Asia, Africa, and Latin America, has also played a role in the shift in global power dynamics. These countries have experienced rapid economic growth and have risen to prominence in the global economy. They've also expanded their political clout through regional organizations like the African Union and the Association of Southeast Asian Nations (ASEAN). The IBSA alliance was formed by India, Brazil, and South Africa to

increase their influence
on global governance.

CHAPTER 4

Implications for the Global Order.

The global power dynamics shift has far-reaching consequences for the global order. It is challenging Western powers' traditional dominance in the global economy, politics, and security. It has also increased competition for resources, markets, and influence among nations. China's rise, in particular, has raised concerns about its intentions and the prospect of conflict with the US. The decline of Western powers has raised concerns about the future of the transatlantic alliance and the United States' ability to maintain global leadership.

Conclusion

The shift in global power dynamics is a multifaceted and complex phenomenon. It is fueled by a confluence of economic, political, and military factors, including China's rise, the decline of Western powers, and the rise of developing nations. The global implications of this shift are significant and far-reaching. They include increased international competition, challenges to Western powers' traditional dominance, and the possibility of conflict between rising and established powers. The future of the global order will be determined by how nations navigate

these changes and their
ability to collaborate to
address common
challenges.